# REPEATING PATTERNS
## COLORING BOOK

# 101 UNIQUE DESIGNS

### By Mary Robertson

# Repeating Patterns
## Coloring Book
## 101 Unique Designs

by Mary Robertson

**JUMEAUX**™

Published by Jumeaux Media, LLC
Las Cruces, New Mexico, USA

ISBN  978-1-938519-13-0

**Library of Congress Subject Headings:**

Repetitive Patterns (Decorative Arts)
Coloring Books
Design

This coloring book is suitable for colored pencils, markers, and gel pens. Placing an extra sheet of paper between pages will help control bleed-through if using alcohol-based design markers. Copies are permitted for personal use.

For ages 12 and up.

Happy coloring!

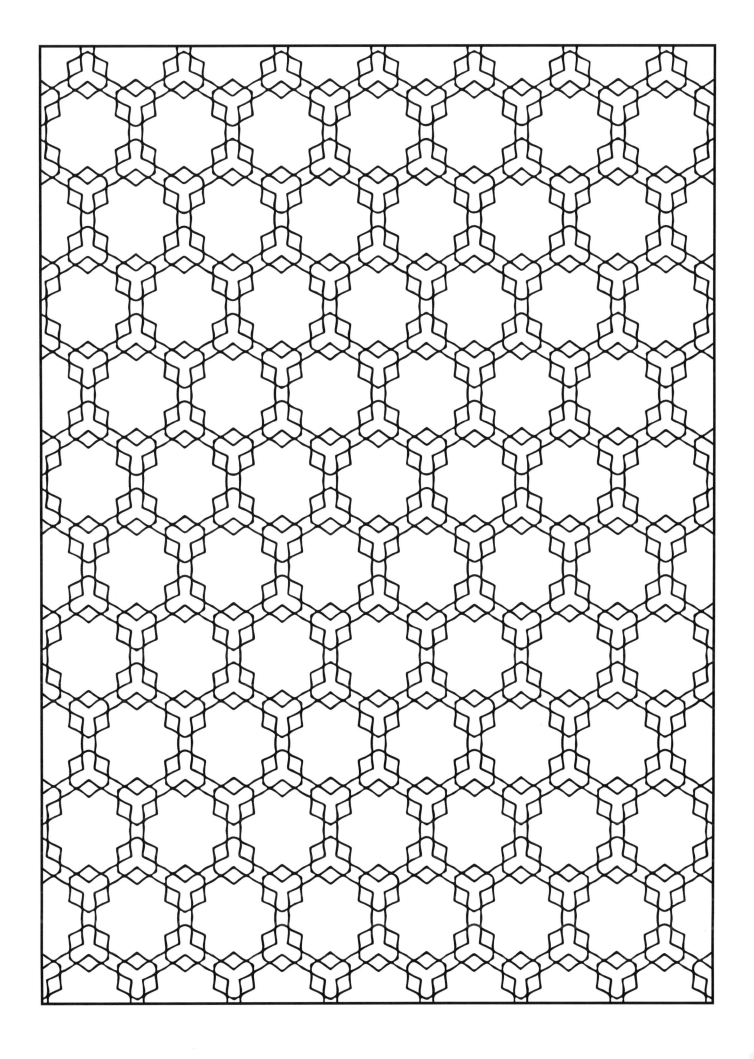

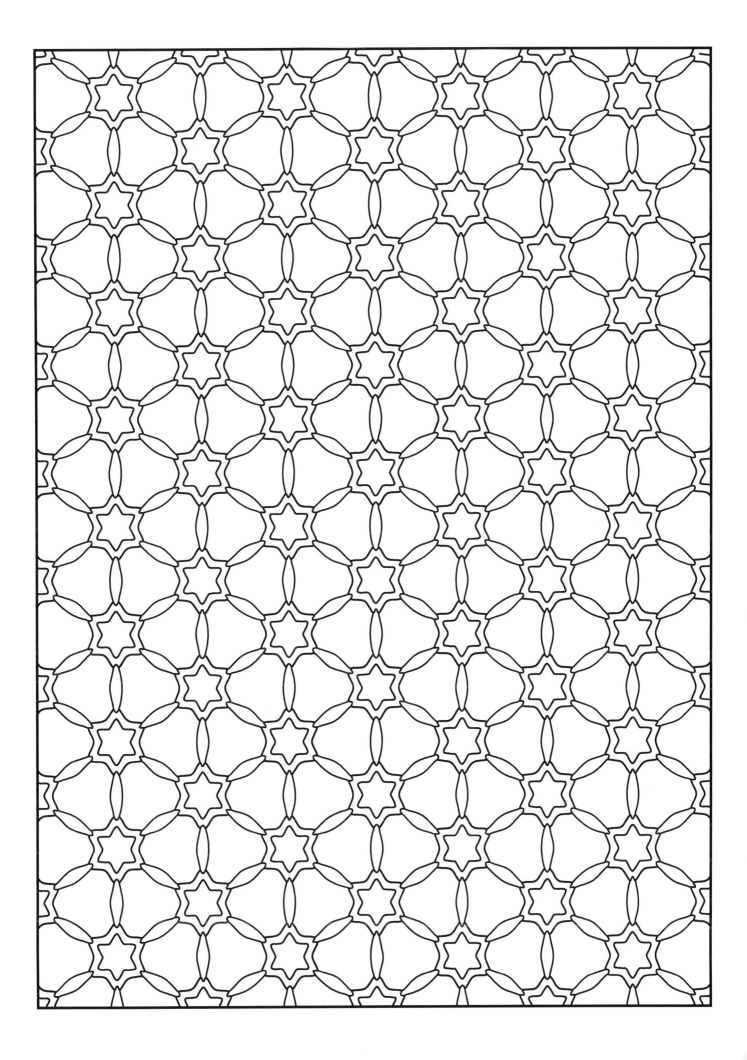

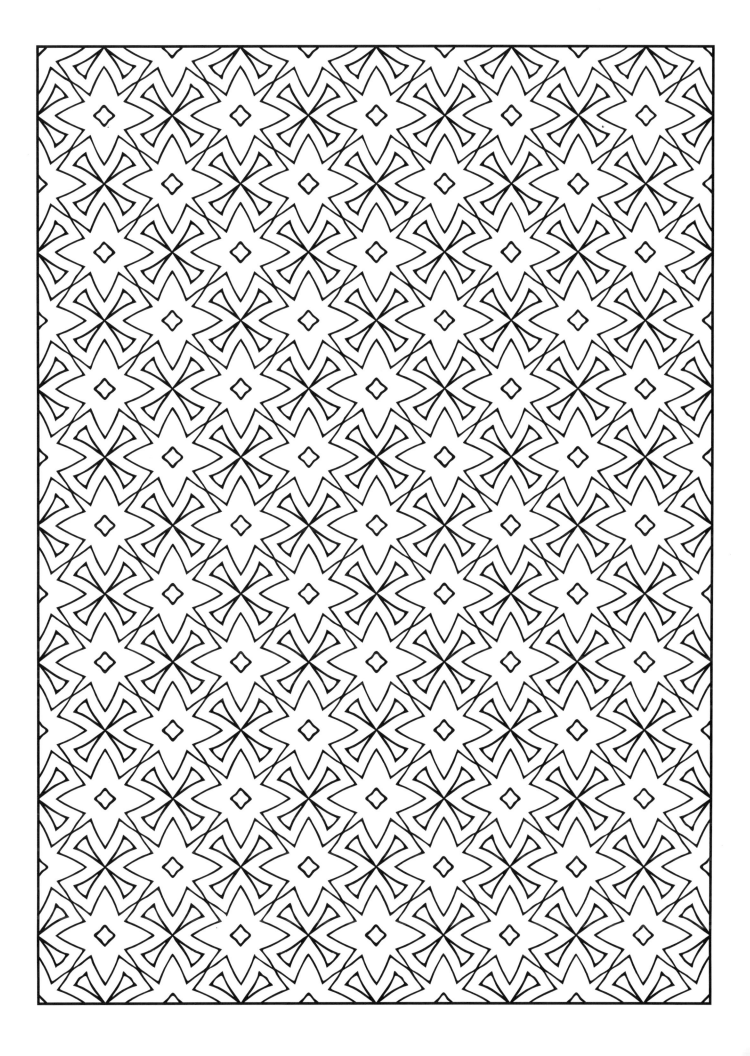

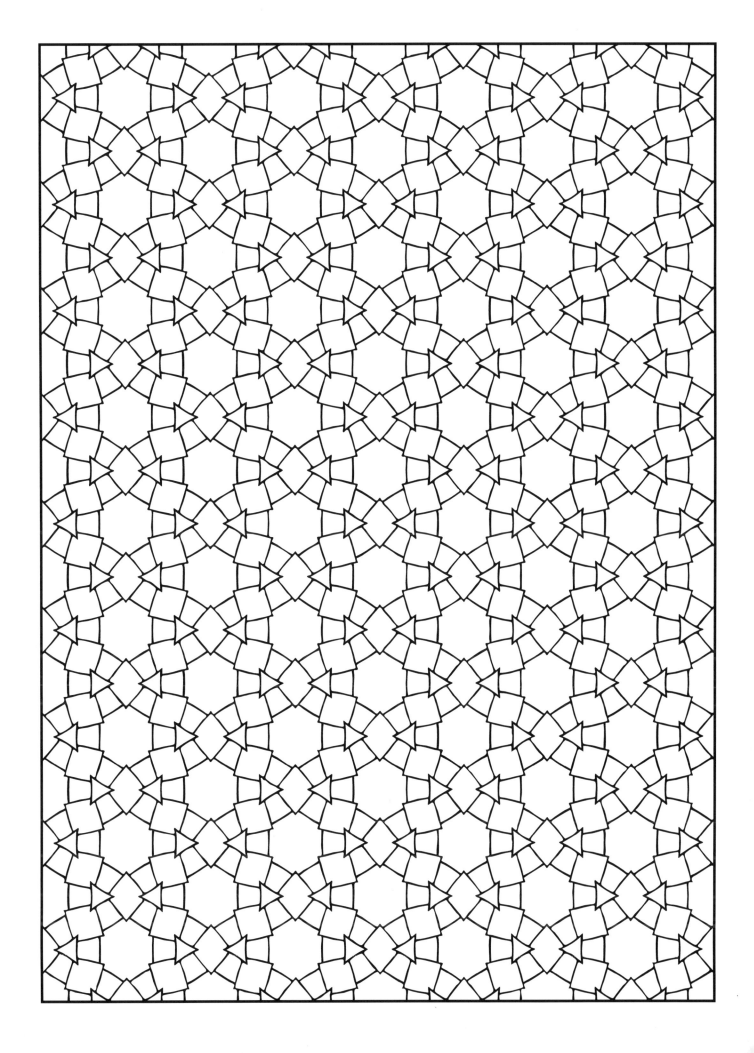

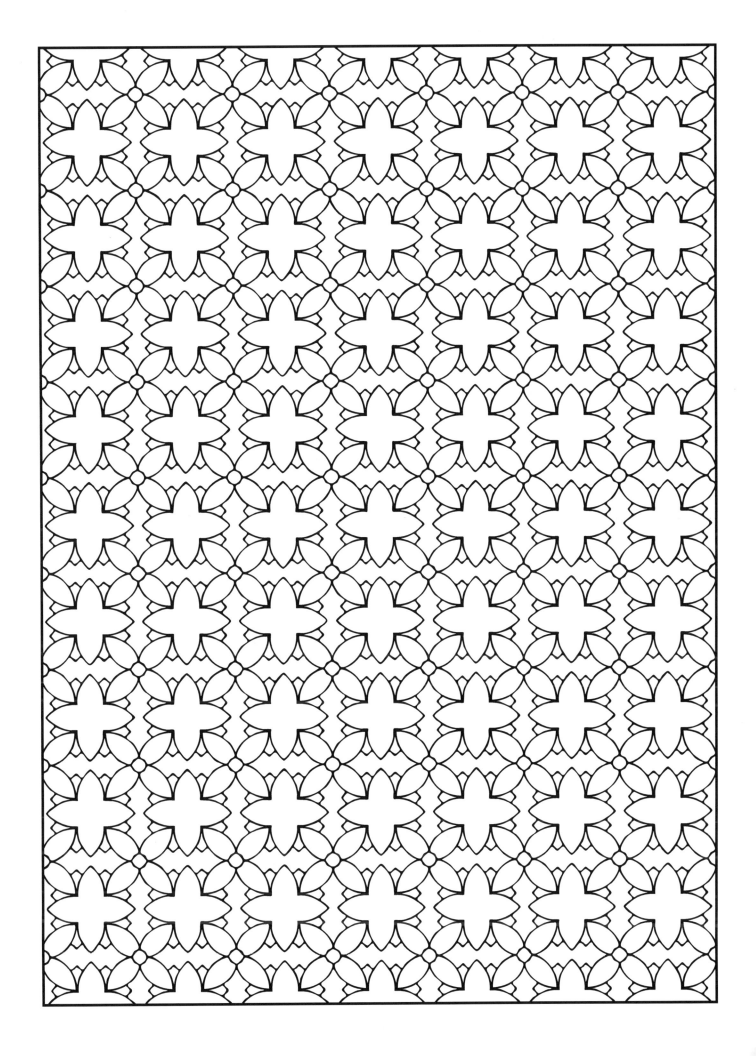

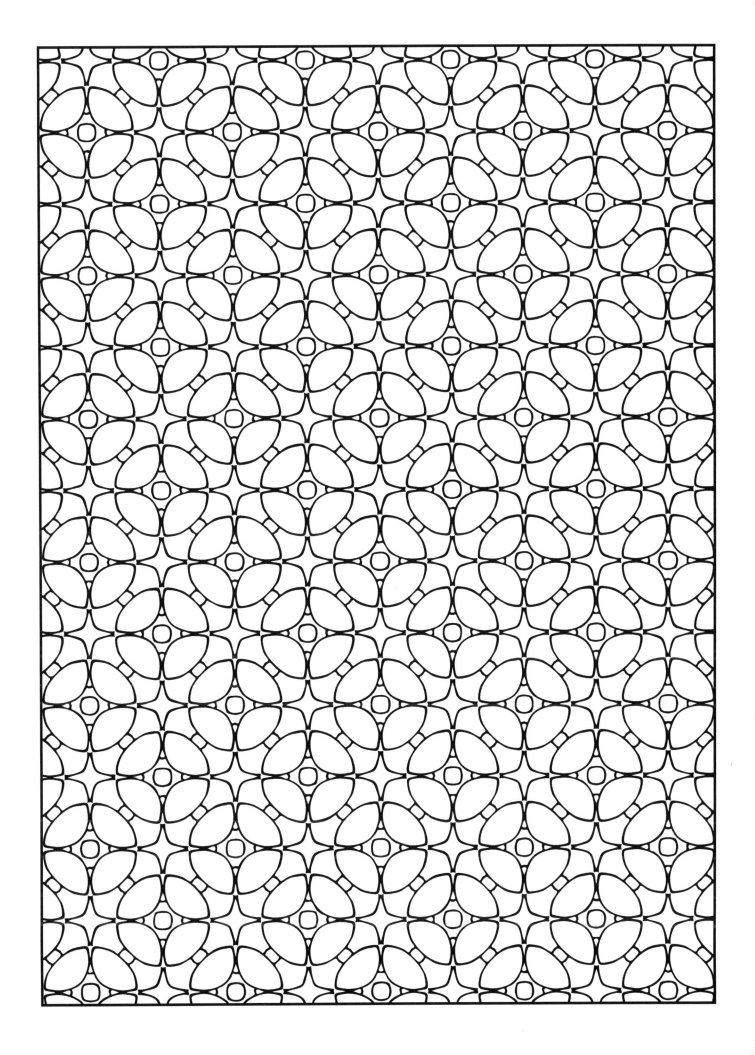

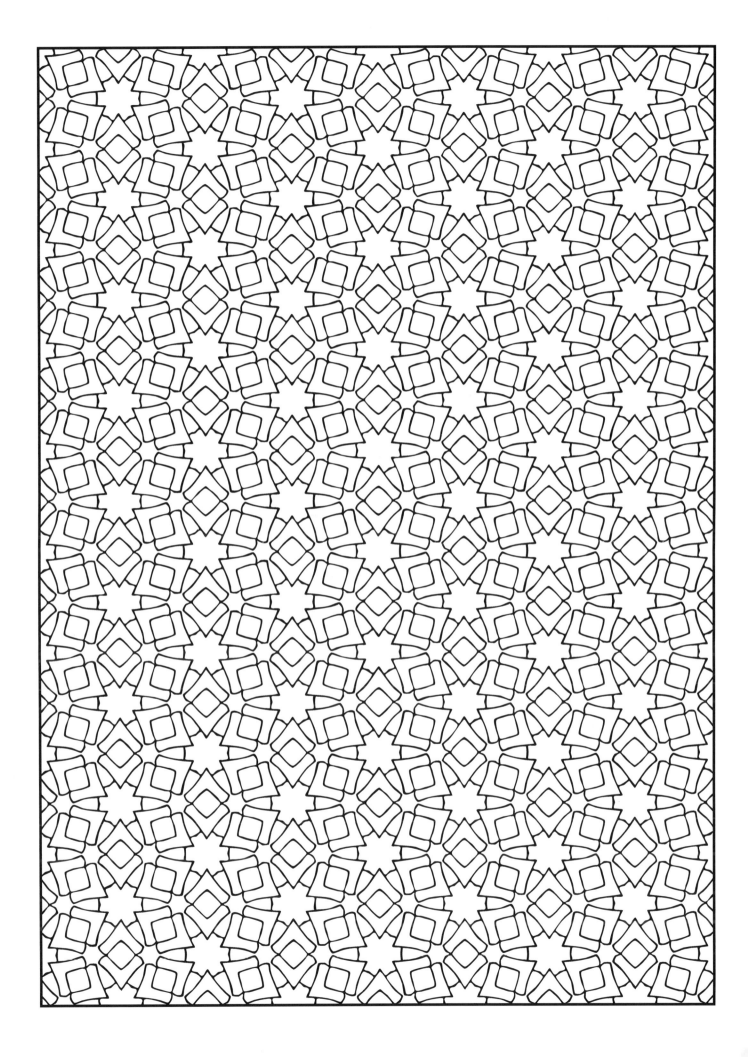

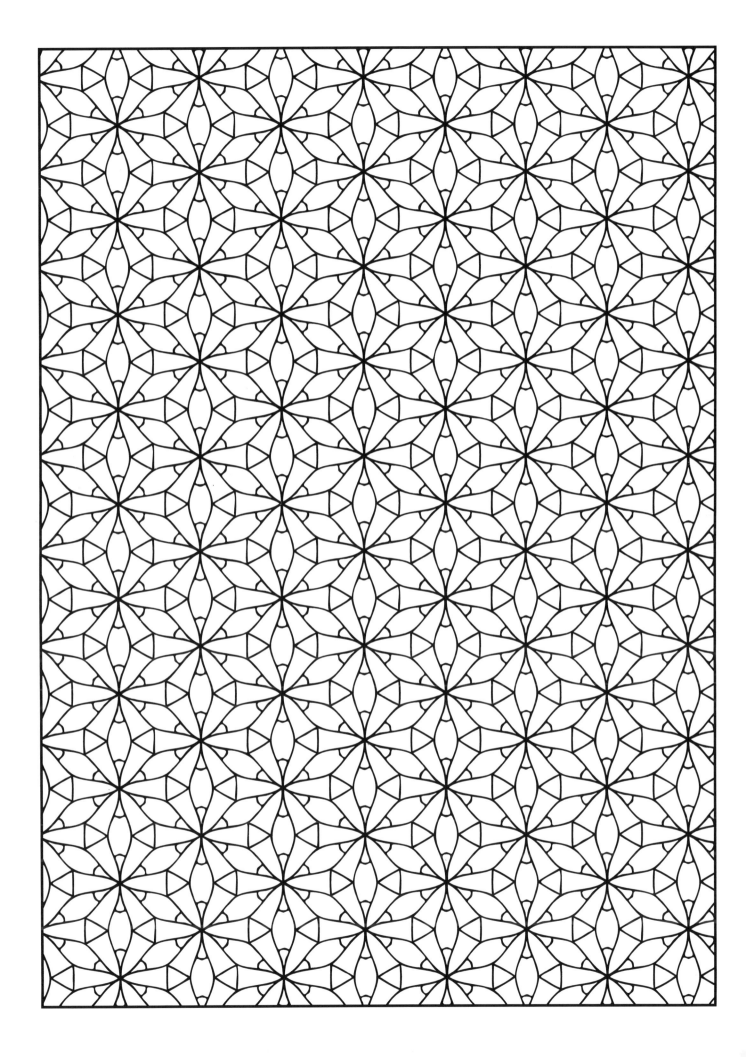

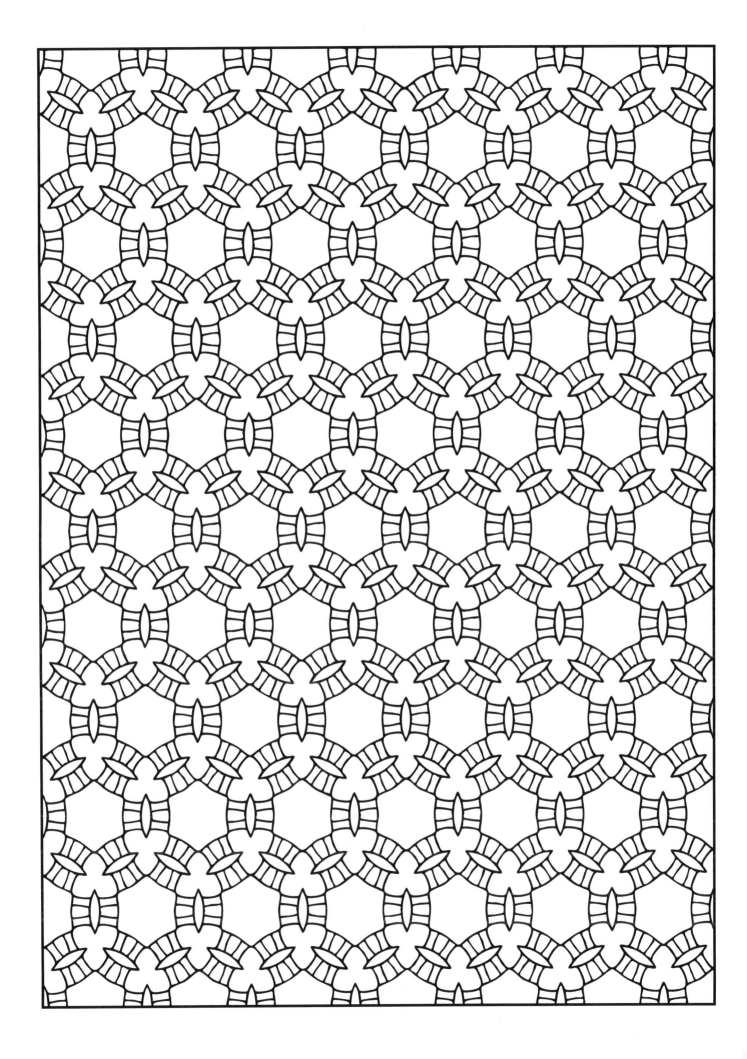

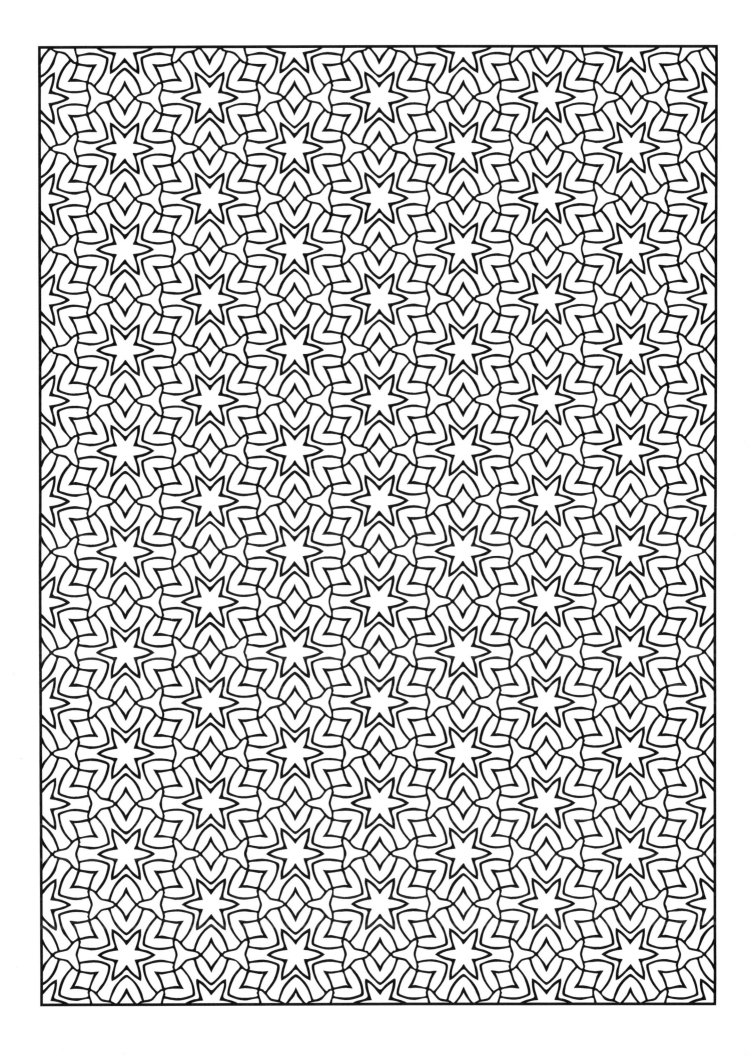

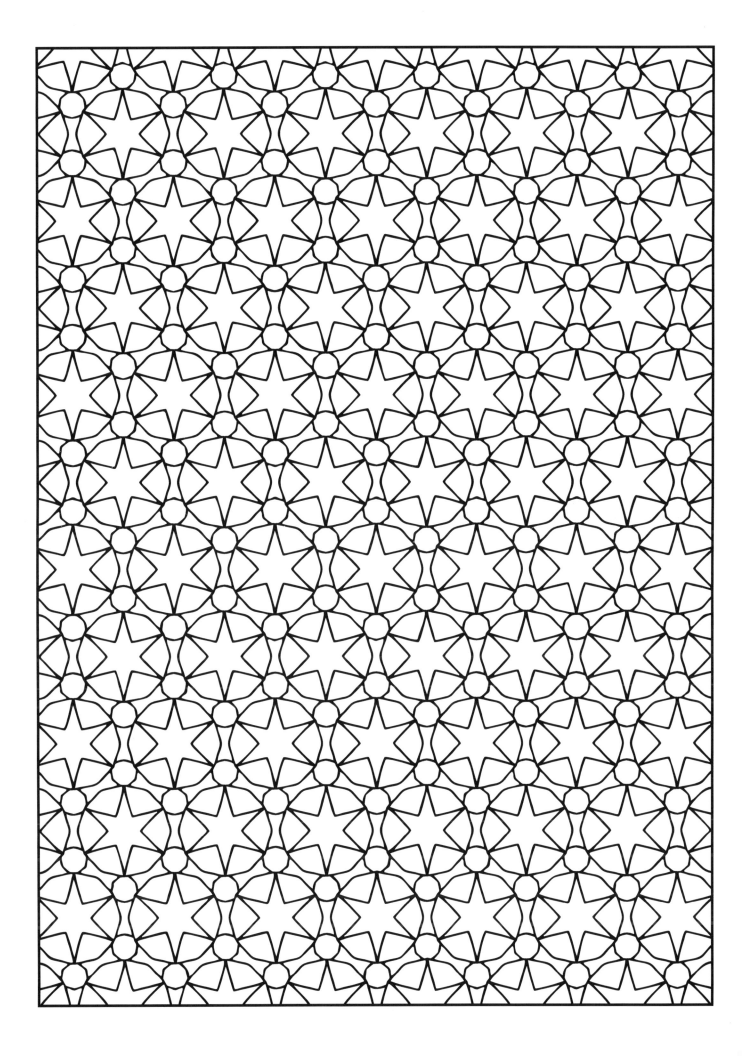

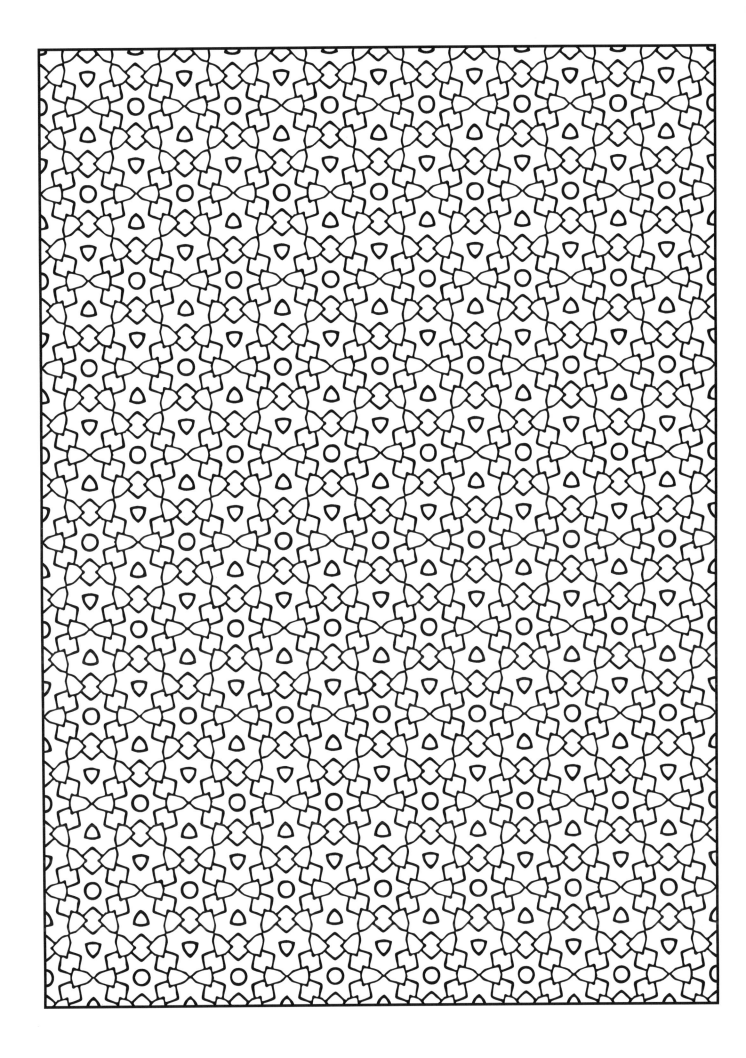

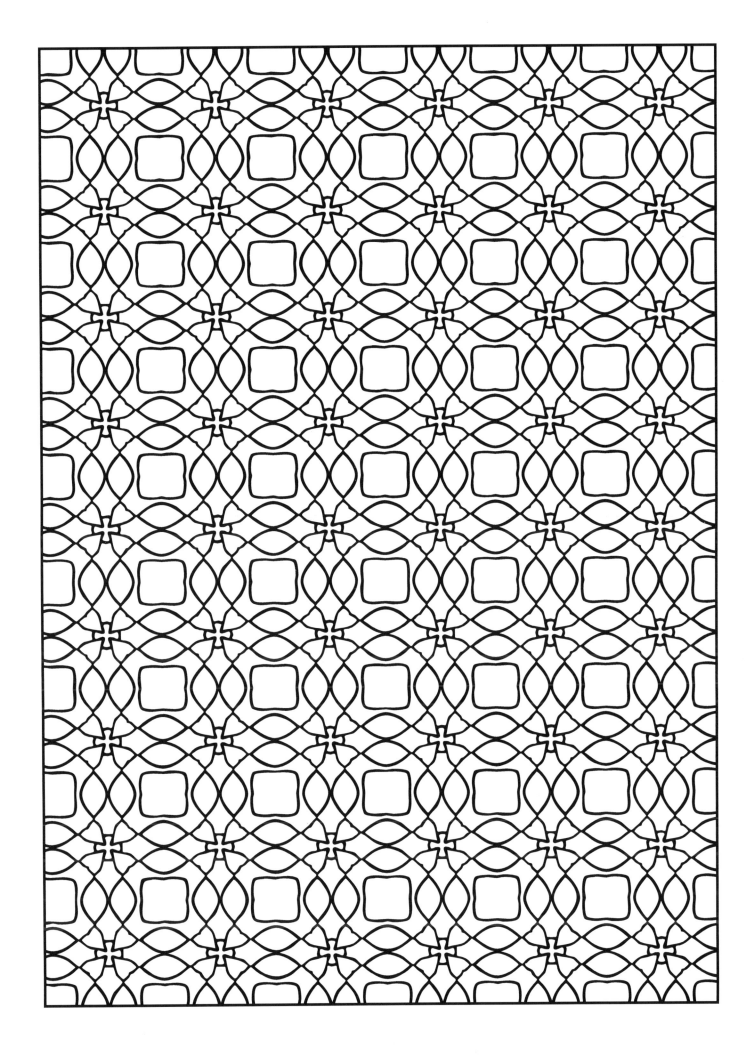

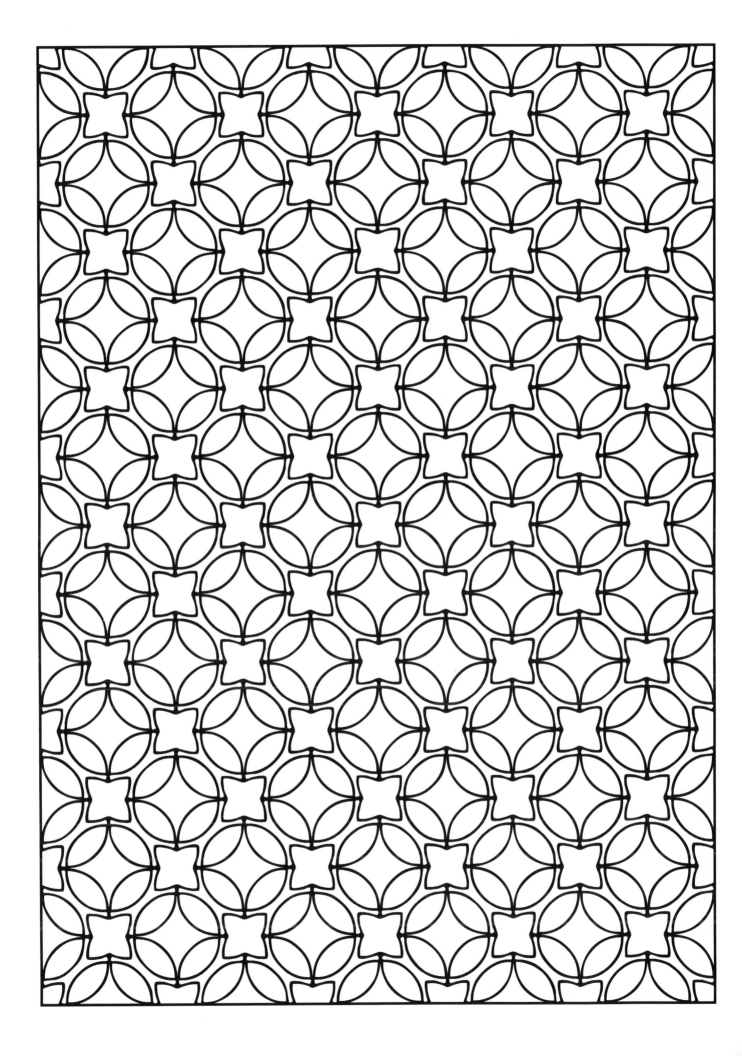

JUMEAUX™

# Coloring Books from Jumeaux Media, LLC

By Mary Robertson:
~Mandalas (Volume 1)  50 original mandala illustrations, all hand drawn.
~Mandalas (Volume 2)  50 more hand drawn mandala designs.
~Mandalas (Volume 3)  50 all new hand drawn mandala designs.
~Mandalas (Volume 4)  50 new original mandala designs to color.
~Mandalas (Volume 5)  50 all new hand drawn mandala designs.
~Kaleidoscope Mandalas (Volume 1) 50 kaleidoscopic mandala designs.
~Kaleidoscope Mandalas (Volume 2) 50 more kaleidoscopic mandalas.
~Mini Mandalas (Volume 1) 200 miniature mandala drawings for coloring.
~Mandala Designs (Volume1) 101 easy mandalas for creative coloring.
~Twisted Tessellations Coloring Book: 50 Unique Designs

About the author and illustrator:

Mary Robertson lives in New Mexico with her husband and two daughters.  She holds a BFA in Painting and Drawing from the University of New Mexico. Examples of Mary's artwork can be seen at: www.maryrobertson.us

Made in the USA
Middletown, DE
30 April 2015